RHIANNON
DAUGHTER OF
NEFEYDD

The Mythology of the Sacred Land

To the early Celts, the land was a living entity, peopled with mysterious and magical beings, and each place had its own story, its own fragment of the great mythology of the land. In Ireland, there still exists a huge collection of ancient topographical stories, known as *Dindshenchas* (Landlore), that relate the mythology of the land itself – its trees, hills, rivers and cliffs, each with its own tale of magic – and of the gods, goddesses and heroes of the Celtic people.

However, it is in their myths and legends that the sacred nature of the land is reflected, often given shape and form in stories of Otherworldly women who represent the soul of the land. Again and again we read of would-be kings who seek to establish a relationship with the land over which they are to rule by marrying the women who represent the sovereignty of the land. This is a particularly strong theme in Irish myth, as, for example, in the story of Niall of the Nine Hostages. As a youth, Niall is tested for his fitness to rule when he encounters a hideous woman by a well. It is only when he brings himself to kiss her that she reveals herself as Ériu, the Sovereignty of Ireland, and turns into a beautiful woman whom Niall eventually marries – at the same time symbolically wedding himself to the land.

Such stories underlie a large part of Celtic mythology and serve to emphasize the spiritual links with the land that were once common to all human beings. Echoes of these links can be found in the rocks and standing stones, the ancient trackways and, above all, in the tales which still surround both natural and man-made sites in every corner of these lands.

These memorials tell, for example, of the burial place of Branwen, daughter of Llŷr, by the lonely shores of Anglesey or recount how a group of people dancing on the Sabbath were turned to stone and became the Rollright Stones in Oxfordshire. Other sites are known to be Faery hills, which, at certain times of the year, act as gateways to the Otherworld.

A *foot-shaped hollow in this rock near Corwen, in Wales, is said to have been made by the Welsh hero Owen Glyndwr.*

Lia-Fáil *(The Stone of Destiny) at the Mound of Hostages, Tara, in County Meath, Ireland.*

The Eildon Hills on the borders of Scotland and England are remembered as the place where Thomas the Rhymer, magician, prophet and poet, met the Queen of Faery and where, centuries later, the Reverend Robert Kirk vanished from mortal sight in his pursuit of the Faery race which he had studied for most of his life.

Everywhere in the lands settled by the Celts there are springs, hills, stones and other natural features that have been rendered sacred through age-old celebrations of the relationship between human beings and the Earth.

The Paps of Anu in County Kerry, Ireland, are said to represent the breasts of the goddess of that name who guards the fertility of the land.

At Alderley Edge in Cheshire, the face of the enchanter Merlin looks out from the cliff-face above a mysterious fountain.

Brightly coloured cloths, called 'cluties', decorate a tree growing over the ancient Madron's Well in Cornwall. Pilgrims tie them onto the tree with a prayer.

Gods & Goddesses

THE EARLY CELTS SAW DEITY – in the form of trees, rivers, lakes and mountains – as a manifestation of the natural world. They only began to make semi-human images of their gods and goddesses after encountering the Classical traditions of Greece and Rome. However, although there is no clearly defined pantheon of Celtic deities, we do find a Father, Mother, Son and Daughter – a family of deities, like a human family.

In Ireland, the role of the Father is fulfilled by the Dagda, or 'Good God', a figure of immense energy and strength, alternately characterized as wise and generous or uncouth and gluttonous. The Welsh equivalent is Brân the Blessed (Bendigeid Vran), regarded as supreme guardian and dispenser of knowledge and wisdom, particularly through the power of story.

In Welsh tradition, the figures of the Mother and Son – Modron and Mabon – are shadowy. 'Modron' and 'Mabon' are titles rather than names: Modron, the Divine Mother, encompasses all the goddesses, while Mabon, the Divine Child, is the guardian of all young people. The Triple Mother Goddess(es) in Celtic tradition are known as the Matronae and dedications to them are found all over the Celtic world. The Daughter is Creiddylad, who, as the Spring Maiden, becomes the subject of an age-long battle between the Kings of Summer and Winter. The winner receives the hand of the Spring Maiden, and thus the turning of the Wheel of the Year is assured.

In addition, there are the gods and goddesses who reign over aspects of the natural world. In Welsh myth, Rhiannon represents the strength of the earth, while the goddess Arianrhod rules over the stars from her fortress of Caer Siddi. Arawn, the dark-natured, crafty Lord of the Underworld,

This carving depicts the three Matronae, or Mothers, the triple goddesses of the Celtic world, who represent both human fertility and the fertility of the Earth.

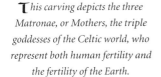

The Goddess Epona marks the great devotion towards horses that is shared by most of the Celtic peoples.

4

The MYTHOLOGY of the SACRED LAND

TO THE EARLY CELTS, the land was a living entity, peopled with mysterious and magical beings, and each place had its own story, its own fragment of the great mythology of the land. In Ireland, there still exists a huge collection of ancient topographical stories, known as *Dindshenchas* (Land-lore), that relate the mythology of the land itself – its trees, hills, rivers and cliffs, each with its own tale of magic – and of the gods, goddesses and heroes of the Celtic people.

However, it is in their myths and legends that the sacred nature of the land is reflected, often given shape and form in stories of Otherworldly women who rep-resent the soul of the land. Again and again we read of would-be kings who seek to establish a relationship with the land over which they are to rule by marrying the women who represent the sovereignty of the land. This is a particularly strong theme in Irish myth, as, for example, in the story of Niall of the Nine Hostages. As a youth, Niall is tested for his fitness to rule when he encounters a hideous woman by a well. It is only when he brings himself to kiss her that she reveals herself as Ériu, the Sovereignty of Ireland, and turns into a beautiful woman whom Niall eventually marries – at the same time symbolically wedding himself to the land.

Such stories underlie a large part of Celtic mythology and serve to emphasize the spiritual links with the land that were once common to all human beings. Echoes of these links can be found in the rocks and standing stones, the ancient trackways and, above all, in the tales which still surround both natural and man-made sites in every corner of these lands. These memorials tell, for example, of the burial place of Branwen, daughter of Llŷr, by the lonely shores of Anglesey or recount how a group of people dancing on the Sabbath were turned to stone and became the Rollright Stones in Oxfordshire. Other sites are known to be Faery hills, which, at certain times of the year, act as gateways to the Otherworld.

Lia-Fáil (The Stone of Destiny) at the Mound of Hostages, Tara, in County Meath, Ireland.

A foot-shaped hollow in this rock near Corwen, in Wales, is said to have been made by the Welsh hero Owen Glyndwr.

This ancient stone from Boa Island, Lough Erne, County Fermanagh, is one of the oldest depictions of deity to be found in Ireland.

This detail from the Gundestrup Cauldron, which was discovered in a bog in Denmark, depicts one of the gods that were worshipped by the Gaulish Celts.

...been linked ...world.

...eaten, ...which, ...eities that the Celts ...with the natural world, ...turning of the seasons and celeb- ...presence of the divine in all things.

Heroes

Heroic tales and legends comprise a large part of Celtic literature, which is not surprising because the Celts were a warrior people who loved fighting for its own sake.

In Ireland, the greatest heroes were the Red Branch Knights of Ulster, particularly Cúchulainn, while both Ireland and Scotland share the great warrior–poet Fionn mac Cumhaill (Finn mac Cool). Cycles of stories tell of the wondrous births, fantastic adventures, wild loves and strange deaths of this pair, many of whose adventures centred around Navan Fort (*Emain Macha*) in Armagh and the Hill of Allen (*Almu*) in Kildare.

Cúchulainn, whose birth name was Sétanta, gained his adult name after killing the fierce hound of Conchobar mac Nessa's smith, Culann. In recompense for the loss, Sétanta agreed to guard Culann's forge until a suitable dog could be found – and thus became Cúchulainn (Hound of Culann). He was famed for his great skills: the salmon leap, which enabled him to leap over obstacles, and his use of *Gae Bulga* – a terrible spear which inflicted a death blow whenever it was used. He was also renowned for his battle frenzy, in which state his body contorted itself horribly, blood spurted from his head in a great gush and his anger was unquenchable unless a host of women were sent to minister to him.

Branwen's Messenger by Margaret Jones. Branwen, daughter of Llyr, was given in marriage to the King of Ireland, who mistreated her. A tame starling took a message to her brother, who came to her rescue.

This detail from the Gundestrup Cauldron shows dead warriors being placed in the Cauldron of Rebirth, from whence they emerged, restored but struck dumb.

The Grave of Taliesin (Bedd Taliesin), *on the shores of Lake Bala in Wales, is
believed to be the resting place of the great 6th-century bard.*

Fionn mac Cumhaill was fostered by a druidess called
Bodhmall and Liath Luachra, a woman-warrior who taught him
battle skills and the arts. Under the name of Demne, he learned poetry
from the druid Finnéces and, in the process, gained the ability to see the
future by eating of the Salmon of Knowledge. In due time he became head
of the Fianna, an elite fighting force that protected Ireland from its
enemies. He was briefly married to the lovely Gráinne, but he was by far
the older and she eloped with the handsome warrior Diarmait. Fionn
pursued the pair and brought about the death of Diarmait, who faded
away into the Otherworld.

In Wales, King Arthur and his band of heroes were the most
frequent subjects of story and myth, although their rough and often
savage ways were a far cry from the chivalrous medieval tales of the
Knights of the Round Table. Among the 150 heroes of Arthur's war-
band were men whose skills were decidedly Otherworldly: Cei, for
instance, who was the model for Sir Kay in English Arthurian
romance, could hear an ant getting up in the morning five
miles (eight kilometres) away, while Sgilti Lightfoot was so
swift that he could run on the tops of the grass and Gilla
Stag-Shank could leap over three fields at a single bound.
The legends of Arthur are founded on the wonderful
richness and invention of the Celtic storytellers, and
many of the stories that became world-famous in the
Middle Ages originated in the time of the Celts.

Voyages

THROUGHOUT CELTIC TRADITION, magical places are seen to lie 'over the sea', 'through the circle' or 'at the World's End'. A whole genre of works, known in Irish as *Imrama* (Voyages), was devoted to journeys to these places. The voyages of Bran mac Febail, Máel Dúin, St Brendan and Mac Conglinne, among others, take the form of visits to a series of islands which represent stages on the soul's journey. The heroes of these stories and poems learn from the experience, encountering gods, spirits and wondrous creatures who exist both to challenge and instruct.

Thus we find Bran mac Febail meeting a wonderful Faery woman who shakes a branch of silver hung with golden apples to send him forth on his adventure, while Máel Dúin, on his voyage, encounters a veritable menagerie of curious beasts, strange beings, and wondrous Otherworldly people on each island.

Other notable voyages are those of Snegdus and Mac Riagla, which begins as a quest for vengeance and ends when the heroes are transformed by the wonders of the islands that they visit, and of *Ua Corra* (the sons of Corra), who undertake their venture as a penance for their misspent youth!

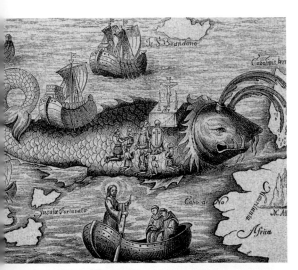

The story of Brendan's Voyage describes how the saint and his men made camp on the back of a gigantic sea creature, probably a whale.

Brandon's Creek in County Kerry, Ireland, is traditionally the place where St Brendan the Navigator began his voyage in search of the Otherworld.

Perhaps the most famous is that of St Brendan. In this, the saint learns of an earlier voyage in search of the Land of Youth and sets out to follow the same route. On the way he encounters the great whale Jasconius, on whose back he and his followers camp overnight. They visit the Island of Ageless Elders and the Island of Birds but, although they come close to the Land of Youth, they are not permitted to go ashore.

An account of another wonderful voyage comes not from a Celtic source but from a Classical Roman description of Britain, which those living elsewhere often perceived as being not unlike the Otherworld. When the historian and geographer Procopius describes the island that he called 'Brittia', he makes it clear that this is no ordinary place and tells how the fishermen of Brittany are called upon to ferry the dead across the sea to Cornwall. Although they can see nothing of their passengers, their boats are heavy on the way out but light and empty on the way home.

The tradition of the great voyage has continued to intrigue ever since. Writers as diverse as Samuel Taylor Coleridge, in his 'Rime of the Ancient Mariner', and C.S. Lewis, in his *Voyage of the Dawn Treader*, have drawn upon these ancient Celtic stories, while the adventures of the USS *Enterprise* in Gene Roddenbury's *Star Trek* take the voyage still further – out into the stars.

Tristan and Isolde, by John Duncan, shows the two famous Celtic lovers about to drink a love potion while on a voyage from Ireland to Cornwall.

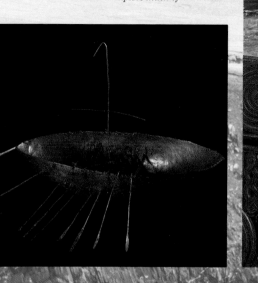

This wonderful golden boat from Ireland is a replica of one of the ships which early Celtic navigators used to explore much of the world.

Quests

LIKE THE VOYAGES TO OTHER WORLDS, quests for sacred or mysterious objects are also a popular subject among Celtic storytellers, probably the most famous being the quest for the Grail. Later medieval accounts focus on the search for spiritual treasure by the Knights of the Round Table but, in the earliest reference, King Arthur himself leads a raid on the Underworld of Annwn, sailing with a band of heroes in his magical ship *Prydwen* in quest of a magical life-restoring cauldron. The poet Taliesin left a mysterious account of this in one of his poems, part of which reads:

Right: Bardsey island, off the coast of Wales, is traditionally the place to which Merlin retired, taking with him the Thirteen Treasures of Britain.

> *... my song sounded*
> *In the four-towered Caer, forever turning,*
> *And of its Cauldron was my first song sung.*
> *Nine maidens kindled it with their breath –*
> *Of what nature is the Lord of Annwn's*
> *Cauldron?*
> *Enamelled iridescence and pearly white its rim.*
> *It will not boil the coward's portion ...*
> *When we went with Arthur – splendid labour –*
> *Except seven, none returned from the Caer of*
> *the Honey-Mead.*

Such cauldrons were common in Celtic myth and could dispense anything from inspiration to food for heroes. A Welsh manuscript contains a catalogue of mysterious, much sought-after treasures – the Thirteen Treasures of Britain – including:

- Dyrnwyn, the Sword of Rhydderch the Generous, which, in the hands of a nobleman, bursts into flame from hilt to tip.
- The Hamper of Gwyddno Garanhir, into which food for one man can be placed and food for a hundred will be found when it is next opened.
- The Horn of Bran Galed, which dispenses whatever drink is desired.

All Thirteen Treasures reveal a preoccupation with the worthiness of the person finding or using them; they will not work for the unworthy. According to an old legend, Merlin is believed to have been the guardian of the Treasures, and to have taken them with him when he retired to the island of Bardsey, off the coast of Wales. There he built an invisible tower of glass, in which he bides still, protecting the Treasures from the eyes of curious seekers.

The Voyage to Annwn, *by Miranda Gray, shows Arthur and seven heroes braving the sea serpent which guards the Otherworldly kingdom.*

Pendragon Castle in Cumbria is *believed to have been the original home of Uther, father of King Arthur, and local tradition tells of hidden treasure.*

The Faery World

THE FAERY PEOPLE OCCUPIED A PLACE OF GREAT IMPORTANCE FOR THE CELTS, who saw them, if not as gods, then as descendants of gods. Some called them the *Tuatha Dé Danann*, or Children of Dana, who was one of the oldest gods of Ireland. Others saw them as one of the aboriginal races of Britain, representative of an older way of communion with the natural world – a way which did not seek to control or manipulate it by the use of iron, a metal traditionally inimical to the Faery folk.

For many people, they are the Sídhe, the people of the Hollow Hills, who dwell beneath the earth in palaces roofed with gold and wield a wild and unpredictable magic. Descriptions of them paint a portrait of beings larger than life: tall, fair and terrible. As the poet Fiona MacLeod wrote:

> *How beautiful they are,*
> *The Lordly Ones,*
> *Who live in the hills,*
> *In the Hollow Hills.*

Faery hills, mounds, trees and springs are found everywhere across the landscapes of Ireland, Scotland, Wales and Brittany, marking hundreds of ways into (but not always out of) the Faery realms. Numerous stories tell of encounters with the Faery folk: midwives called upon to nurse Faery children; human children exchanged for Faery offspring; musicians asked to play at Faery banquets; and treasure-seekers falling by accident into Faery mounds – either never to be seen again or emerging changed forever.

The Faery tradition of the Celts remains one of the richest in the world, with hundreds of tales set in a world where anything can happen: where heroes can grow overnight to such a size that their feet stick out of the window of the house; where animals

The Faery Woman Summons Connla, *by Ian Daniels. The hero Connla is summoned to the land of the Sídhe by a mysterious Faery woman.*

Bryn-celli-ddu, *on the island of Anglesey, has strong associations with the Faery people, as well as containing some of the oldest and most mysterious of any carvings found elsewhere in the British Isles.*

talk and know more than humans; where beauty is often synonymous with danger, as those who pursue Faery women find to their cost. Throughout much of the Celtic world, many people still believe in the Faery people. As one collector of Celtic Faery lore, Jeremiah Curtin, remarked:

> When I was a boy ... nine men in ten believed in fairies, and said so; now only one man in ten will say that he believes in them. If one of the nine believes, he will not tell you; he will keep his mind to himself.

The perilous, shining Faery realm underlies much of Celtic myth and legend, occasionally spilling over into this world, which is always the richer for the contact.

The Reverend Robert Kirk was believed to have vanished into a Faery hill in the 18th century. This site at Aberfoyle, near Stirling in Scotland, may be his final resting place.

13

Legendary & Mythic Sites in the British Isles

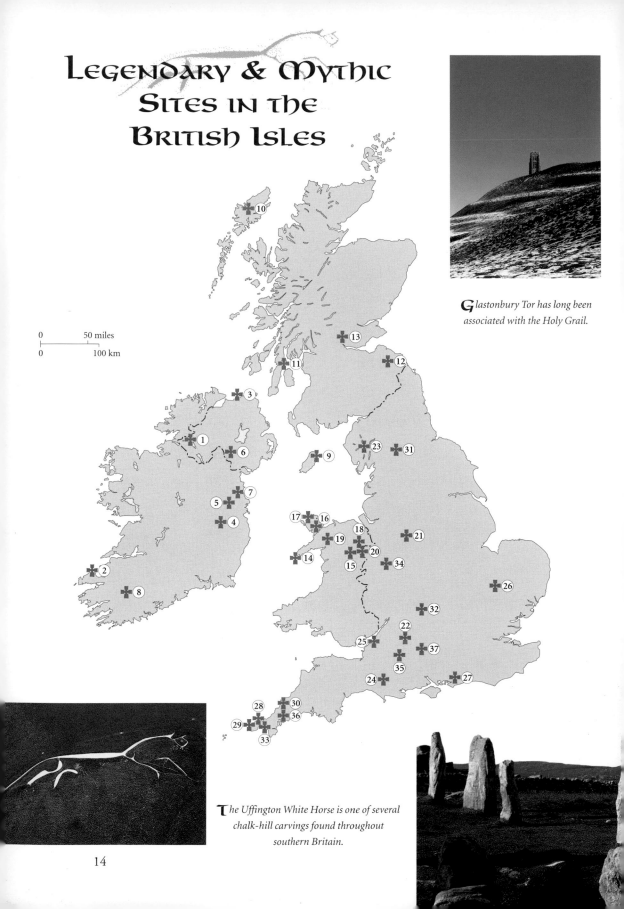

Glastonbury Tor has long been associated with the Holy Grail.

0   50 miles
0   100 km

10
13
11
12
3
1
6
23
31
9
5
7
4
17   16
18
19
14
20
15
34
21
2
8
26
32
22
25
37
35
24
27
28   30
29   36
33

The Uffington White Horse is one of several chalk-hill carvings found throughout southern Britain.

Ireland

1. Boa Island, Lough Erne, Fermanagh
2. Brandon's Creek, Kerry
3. Giant's Causeway, Antrim
4. Hill of Allen *(Almu)*, Kildare
5. Hill of Tara, Meath
6. Navan Fort *(Emain Macha)*, Armagh
7. Newgrange *(Brug na Bóinne)*, Meath
8. Paps of Anu, Kerry

Isle of Man

9. Maughold's Head

Scotland

10. Callanish Standing Stones, Lewis, Western Isles
11. *Carraig-an-Taláidh*, near Skipness, Strathclyde
12. Eildon Hills, Borders
13. Faery Hill, Aberfoyle, Stirling

The Standing Stones of Callanish, on the island of Lewis, are aligned with the rising and setting of the sun.

Wales

14. Bardsey island *(Ynys Enlli)*, Gwynedd
15. Grave of Taliesin *(Bedd Taliesin)*, near Lake Bala, Gwynedd
16. Branwen's Grave, Anglesey
17. *Bryn-celli-ddu*, Anglesey
18. Castle of the Grail (Bran's Fort, *Dinas Bran*), Clwyd
19. Emrys's Fort *(Dinas Emrys)*, Gwynedd
20. Owen Glyndwr's footprint, near Corwen, Clwyd

England

21. Alderley Edge, Cheshire
22. Avebury Stone Circle, Wiltshire
23. Castlerigg Stone Circle, Cumbria
24. Chalice Well and Tor, Glastonbury, Somerset
25. Crick Stone, near Horton, Gloucestershire
26. Giant, Sibton Church, near Bury St Edmunds, Suffolk
27. Long Man, Wilmington, East Sussex
28. Madron's (Modron's) Well, Cornwall
29. Men-an-Tol, Cornwall
30. Merlin's Cave, Tintagel, Cornwall
31. Pendragon Castle, Cumbria
32. Rollright Stones, Oxfordshire
33. St Michael's Mount, Cornwall
34. Stiperstones, Shropshire
35. Stonehenge, Salisbury Plain, Wiltshire
36. Tristan's (Drustan) Stone, Cornwall
37. White Horse, Uffington, Oxfordshire

The OTHERWORLD

DESCRIPTIONS OF THE OTHERWORLD abound in Celtic myth and legend, and all agree on one point: it is a glorious and happy place, filled with laughter and light and an abundance of all things – companionship, food and drink, endless fountains of lore and story. Here the Faery people of the Sídhe hold court and make merry, and the gods dispense wisdom.

The Otherworld is often depicted as lying very close to our own world, with entrances in every thorn bush, stream, hill, forest or rocky slope. In many Celtic tales, people stumble into this magical realm almost by accident, passing the invisible threshold between this existence and the other without realizing, until they discern strange landmarks, such as the Green and Burning Tree, half on fire and half green and leafy, or meet the giant, one-eyed, one-legged herdsman, who watches over a host of creatures, or catch sight of a black-and-white chequered field where sheep change from white to black, or vice versa, as they cross from one colour to the other.

A white animal, such as a deer, may also lead people into an Otherworldly reality and, thus, what begins as an ordinary hunt can end as a series of magical adventures. Thus, when the hero Owain pursues a stag into a mysterious forest he discovers a Black Knight, guarding a revitalizing fountain, whom he challenges and overcomes. He then has to assume the guardianship of the fountain and marry the Otherworldly woman who lives beside it.

*S*elkies were half-human creatures who could change their shape into that of a seal.

*T*he Giant's Causeway stretches between the coastlines of Ireland and Scotland and was believed to have been built by giants.

*T*he Mermaid of Zennor, in Cornwall, lured the local squire's son, who possessed a beautiful singing voice, into her sea-kingdom.

The Lad of the Skin Coverings and the Four-Sided Cup, *by Ian Daniels. King Cormac mac Airt was given a cup which broke when three untruths were uttered in its presence and repaired itself when three truths were then uttered.*

Many stories tell of how people who accidentally pass into the Otherworld acquire strange knowledge or wondrous skills. Thus Thomas the Rhymer gains the art of prophecy while at the court of the Faery Queen and King Cormac mac Airt is given the Four-Sided Cup of Truth – which breaks if a falsehood is uttered but knits together again when the truth is told – when he visits the god Manannán mac Lir.

As a place from which knowledge springs, more has been written about the Underworld than anywhere else. In Welsh tradition, it is ruled over by Arawn and Rhiannon, and, in Irish tradition, by Donn. Although it is sometimes seen as a dimly lit place, haunted by shadows and dreams, there is another side to the Underworld: there are stars shining within the earth that illuminate it with their brightness.

The mystery of the Otherworld and its inhabitants haunts the imagination to this day and has influenced generations of creative people, including writer J.R.R. Tolkien and film director George Lucas. Many descriptions of Middle Earth in *The Lord of the Rings* reflect the Celtic vision of the Otherworld, while the underwater world to which Qui Gon Jinn and his friends journey in *Star Wars: The Phantom Menace* resembles the Underworld of Celtic tradition in many ways.

Giants, like the one in this carving from Sibton Church in Suffolk, were the frequent adversaries of Celtic heroes, especially Fionn mac Cumhaill, who battled with a number of these mighty creatures.

Mysterious Landscapes

Castlerigg Stone Circle in Cumbria, also known as the Keswick Carles. According to local tradition, they are people who were turned into stone because they danced on the Sabbath.

EVERYWHERE IN THE LANDS where the Celts have lived there are mythological signposts. In Ireland, the Hill of Tara was both a religious and political centre where, for centuries, new kings celebrated their sacred marriage to the land. *Brug na Bóinne* (Newgrange), in Meath, is an astonishing complex of Neolithic sacred sites that became a focus for celebrations associated with the Celtic sacred year. In the story of Diarmait and Gráinne, the lovers, fleeing for their lives from Gráinne's angry husband, Fionn mac Cumhaill, slept outdoors at a series of places that are still remembered as 'The Beds of Diarmait and Gráinne'. The whole landscape of the Celtic world is thus peopled with strange and wonderful objects, some natural and others man-made.

Megalithic monuments have acquired their own mythology and legends. In England, the great chalk-hill figures, such as the Wilmington Long Man and the Uffington White Horse, which almost certainly pre-date the arrival of the Celts, also became a focus for sacred practices and

acquired their own stories. According to an early account, Stonehenge was built by Merlin, King Arthur's enchanter, who brought the stones across the sea from Ireland and erected them as a lasting memorial to King Ambrosius. The same account cites the origin of the stones as Africa and emphasizes that water poured over the stones had healing properties – a belief that persisted until the seventeenth century.

Other stones were credited with similar properties. Those at Men-an-Tol, in Cornwall, were said to cure babies of various ailments, while the toothache-relieving properties of the chambered tomb at *Carraig-an-Taláidh*, near Skipness in Strathclyde, is outshone by the Crick Stone, near Horton in Gloucestershire, which is said to cure children of rickets. Rituals connecting stones with childbirth are found from the Orkneys to western Ireland. On the Isle of Man, which is named after the sea god Manannán, Maughold's Head is said to have been created as St Maughold, flying across the sea from Ireland, touched the water with his knee and, to this day, the waters of this area are believed to cure eye ailments.

The catalogue of stories anchored in the landscape includes tales of hidden treasure, of stones which cannot be counted or which move by themselves, and of tombs which become the burial place of countless heroes, from King Arthur to Sir Frances Drake, and which were built by giants, the Devil or the Faery people.

These sites still possess a powerful attraction for us. Accustomed as we are to seeing the surrounding landscape in three dimensions, through the eyes of Celtic tradition we can also see it as a magical place, steeped in legend and peopled by beings of the Otherworld.

Stone Circle at Avebury, Wiltshire.

Merlin's Cave in Cornwall has strong associations with the enchanter. Above it, perched on the rocks, is Tintagel Castle, which is reputed to be the birthplace of Arthur.

Far left: The Stiperstones in Shropshire are believed to have come from the Devil, who let them fall from his pockets as he rushed across the countryside.

Left: The mysterious stone of Men-an-Tol in Cornwall is said to cure sick children if they are passed through the hole.

The
Legacy of
the Celts

THE CULTURE AND TRADITION of the Celts survives not only among their descendants in Ireland, Scotland, Wales, Cornwall and the Isle of Man – who each still speak their own distinct Celtic language – but spreads right around the globe. Music, story and song reconnect us all with the legends of the ancestral Celtic lands and their people.

From all over the world, visitors to the British Isles seek to reawaken memory by walking the ancient roads of their forebears in order to listen to the healing wisdom of springs and lakes, to be inspired by the hills, mountains and forests, and to read and listen to the myths and legends of this wise and warm-hearted people. The beliefs of the Celts, their traditions and rituals, their songs and poems, have affected the very way we think and feel, as well as how we react to the world around us.

The bardic traditions that have preserved the memory of these legends are still an important part of Celtic life. In Ireland, the government recognizes 'the people of the gift' – artists, storytellers and musicians – as cultural treasures. In every Celtic land today, there are competitions in which poets and musicians can be seen and acclaimed as the most accomplished of their people. These modern bards still keep open the Otherworldly doors of vision, singing and telling the myths and legends of their ancestors.

The tradition of respect for the land, its trees and animals, which was such an essential part of Celtic life, shows us that we can still learn from the past. The importance of recognizing our own connection with the land is now more urgent than ever as climatic and other environmental changes result from human neglect of nature. In this respect, the Celtic gods and the Faery people are not merely mythical archetypes but can also be interpreted as the living guardians of the land's health. Thus the power of Celtic lore and tradition continues to hold us in the golden webs of its weaving, preserving an eternal, ever-changing pattern of thought, image and dream.

Stonehenge in Wiltshire was probably designed as a huge cosmic amphitheatre from which the passage of the stars could be observed.